Up Here

Mary Stigall

Mary Stigall

WESTERN REFLECTIONS
PUBLISHING COMPANY

Library of Congress Catalog Card Number: 2002104144

ISBN: 1-890437-69-7

Text and jacket design by SJS Design (Susan Smilanic)

Western Reflections Publishing Company
P.O. Box 1647
Montrose, Colorado 81402

Up Here

Everybody in town

went to the Arts and Crafts Show

so the UPS driver

had to bring the thirty pounds of worms

to the church yard

and ask around.

Only In America, mentioned in "Don't Sweat the Green Beans" was originally published by World Publishing Company in 1958.

Portions of "The Alferd Packer Summer" appeared in *Gunnison Country Magazine* in the summer of 1989.

In 1986 I started writing a column, "Up Here," for the Lake City, Colorado, newspaper, *The Silver World.* The pieces predominantly included my impressions of moving from a city to a very small mountain town and the sorting of values that accompanied that move. Much of this book is based on material from those columns.

THE JOURNEY WAS LONG
BUT THE DESTINATION WAS ALWAYS IN SIGHT

The Flatlanders Arrive

It was August of 1971. I sat in the middle of my kitchen floor in a St. Louis suburb, surrounded by towers of canned goods, peas and peaches carefully separated. Sweat dotted my forehead and ran in sluggish trickles down my chest. Why in heaven's name had I ever agreed to go camping in Colorado? My children, Amy, six, and Steve, eleven, were excited about going any place where we had to take our own food. Their main contribution was thinking of other cans we might add to the stacks. I was trying to get excited, but truthfully I had not the slightest desire to sleep in a tent, cook over an open fire, wash dishes by hand or worry about the kids falling into Lake San Cristobal. I'd much rather send them to the municipal pool where there were lifeguards. After the demanding summer school session I'd just taught, all I wanted to do was vegetate in the air conditioning.

I'd never seen the campground where we were going, but I had been camping with our neighbors who'd picked it. We were definitely in for primitive. They were, of course, from Texas and had visited Lake San Cristobal and the Lake City area many years before and had vowed to return.

"You can shop in Gunnison, the nearest town of any size," they had told us, "but the prices will probably be higher and the choices might be limited. We're taking our own food."

So we packed two weeks' nourishment into the large wooden car top carrier my husband had built and painted bright yellow. Along with the green beans, we also loaded four gallons of Coleman fuel only to discover later that it was fifteen cents cheaper per can in Gunnison than in St. Louis. "Twenty-four unnecessary pounds," my husband, Bob, groaned.

After stopping every few miles across hot and barren Kansas to check the position of the yellow monster over our heads, we finally entered the cool mountains of Colorado. Monarch Pass was breathtakingly beautiful but also quite scary to the flatlander. From the pass we drove on Highway 50 by the meandering stream, hayfields and sprawling ranches of the Gunnison Valley. At Blue Mesa Reservoir, we turned onto Highway 149 and into land that became increasingly arid, barren and dull. On a Sunday afternoon in August, we met only one car between Gunnison and Lake City. Was this their idea of a Texas-size joke? Could there be anything at the end of that road? We began to wonder also why we'd left all the pretty behind.

At a point called "The Gate" - columnar formations that do indeed form entry bluffs - the topography changed abruptly. The highway wound near the Lake Fork of the Gunnison River, and the whole scene suddenly became alpine in nature. Closer toward Lake City, imposing rocks towered above the road as it twisted along the banks of the clear, bustling river. We had to admit that the scenery had indeed changed to pretty.

In 1971, the route along the west side of the lake was a dusty, gravel road. The campsite on the other side was also dusty and, perched as it was on the cliff above the lake, appeared dangerous to a young mother. "Well, we are here, and like it or not, this is our home for a couple of weeks."

That evening as the sun slipped behind the Pinnacles - stark rock formations towering above the lake which we named "The Castles" - we bundled ourselves and children in down coats. Years later, we laugh about that. Acclimatized as we are now, an August evening might still find us at the lake in shorts. In 1971, however, a summer night in Colorado was cold.

And so was the next morning. In a couple of days, however, I had it figured out. If I stayed in the tent, Bob, who always got up early, would bring me a cup of coffee followed by a pan of hot water for sponging. And even more delightful, I discovered that once the sun hit the tent, it created engaging aspen-leaf patterns on the roof.

On the second day we puffed up an impossibly steep trail and, of course, were caught in the afternoon thunderstorm, sans ponchos. It had been so bright and sunny when we'd left camp.

In a few days we went digging in pursuit of whatever treasures time had buried around old mining sites. I'm now offended by the notion of that activity, but it seemed perfectly right at the time, something all the tourists did. When we came back to town, we were so dirty that we wouldn't even go into one of Lake City's old-time saloons. The women wouldn't, that is. Much to our chagrin, we watched our husbands, with dirt-streaked faces and mud-covered jeans, not only go into the Elkhorn for a beer, but we discovered that they had plotted with our two six-year old girls, also dirty and bedraggled, to come into the bar after their daddies, begging them to come home. After playing in the dirt for a number of days, the guys were brave enough to stand under the ice-cold, natural waterfall below the campground, but the women and children eventually rented a shower in town at a local motel for fifty cents. The sheriff operated it. We were a long way from the St. Louis suburbs.

The second week, we deemed ourselves experienced enough for an overnight backpacking trip. We chose Sloan Lake, above American Basin, arguably one of the most beautiful spots on earth. Because the hike from American Basin to Sloan Lake was short enough for children, only about two miles, we foresaw no other problems. Short was one determinant, but grade of ascent should have been another. Nevertheless, we scampered up the steep, rocky trail in an August snowstorm, ponchos flapping (at least we'd brought them this time) and children whining most of the way.

We were well above timberline when it dawned on us that one needs wood to build fires, and where there are no trees, there is no wood. Steve and the other older children scampered back down the trail to confiscate whatever limbs, boards or bark they could find. That night we learned that above 13,000 feet you couldn't even burn Kleenex.

Still determined that our kids would experience it all, in a few days we planned another hike up Engineer Pass. It was only a couple of miles and not nearly as steep as the trek up to Sloan Lake. And we would be on a jeep road, which would make for easier walking than a rocky trail. Whether she was not feeling well from the altitude, exhausted or being contrary, I don't know, but early on, Amy balked, whined and dragged her feet. Again, what had begun as a bright, cloudless day suddenly turned grey and we were soon pelted with rain, then snow. The wind whipped our ponchos in front of our faces, totally obscuring our already limited visibility. Finally realizing that I had to take Amy back down, I decided to offer her a snack box of raisins to help pacify her. The proverbial straw broke the camel's back when she cried that the box was full of worms.

So why do I now live in Colorado? Most of the change in my attitude was gradual, but one moment stands out as my own private epiphany. I was hiking down Henson Creek Road one day when life snapped into focus. One could breathe going downhill; the sky was that shocking deep blue, almost purple behind the peaks. Aspen leaves twirled and chimed, the sparkling creek laughed all the way downhill, that damp-pine smell floated in the air, the mountains suddenly surrounded, guarded and embraced me. My apologies, Paul, but this experience was clearly in the burning bush league.

For several summers, we came back to the same camp spot. One year we reluctantly agreed that we were limiting our children's experiences. Therefore, we planned a trip through southern Civil War sites to complement Steve's current interest. One night before our trip, we were sitting outside trying to see some stars in the polluted urban sky. Could we really let a summer go by without sitting by a campfire and gazing at that sparkling expanse above us? Without wearing down coats in August? Without breathing that crisp, pine-laden air? Without crawling into a sleeping bag in a snug tent?

We informed our children that they would have to see the rest of the world on their own, and they have both done a fine job of doing that.

We not only came back, but we bought land in town and started creating our dream of coming back – to stay.

The Flatlanders Get An Idea

 During these years, my husband, Bob, was developing a sideline business of free-lance photography, partly to help him keep his sanity in his increasingly routine government job. It didn't take a rocket scientist to figure out that nobody in Lake City was selling photographs of the local landscape. Now he loves to say that all he had planned to do was build a little cabin on the town land we'd bought in 1976, retire, hang a few pictures on the wall and casually let it be known that they were for sale. I am, however, a good deal more compulsive and finally declared, "You're either going to be in business or you're not."

We built in 1977 and opened Silver Scene Photography for a few weeks in the summer of 1978. My son Steve, ever the conservative, wanted to call it "Lake City Photo." I was much too romantic for that and insisted that we pick up on the idea that we were located on Silver Street, reflecting the silver mining days, and that "Scene" suggested photography. I don't recall any opinion expressed by our daughter, and Bob couldn't have cared less. All he wanted to do was retire and sell photographs. In 1978 I finagled yet another summer off. Bob had a four-week vacation; Steve and Amy were out of school and had learned from their high school journalism classes how to do basic darkroom work. (I'd taken one course at the university where I taught and quickly declared that it was too much like cooking for me.) By Bob and I splitting our vacations with about a week's overlap, we were off and running.

A few weeks before we'd planned to open, I answered a phone call from a Lake City businessman who had a party interested in renting one of his spaces for an old-time portrait studio.

"I wondered if you were planning to do that in your photo shop? The town's not big enough for two, and I figured you should have first go at it."

It's a good thing he talked to me and not Bob.

"Well, yes, as a matter of fact, we are going to offer costumed, old-time portraits," I assured him.

As a matter of fact, we had talked about it as an idea for the future, but it seemed clear to me that we'd better get our foot in the door right away. During the next few weeks, I haunted garage sales and secondhand stores rounding up costumes and props. I repaired and altered anything that looked remotely like Victorian attire. I scanned catalogs for specialties that I couldn't create; Bob rigged up a lighting system, and we all four beefed up on taking portraits.

Even though it was borderline dishonest, starting the costumed old-time portrait business was one of the best moves we made. For years, it brought customers into the gallery who might otherwise have passed us by. My theatre background worked well for dressing people, getting them into character and making sure they were having fun - even for sometimes gently persuading a reluctant dad or grandma to join in the posing. The kids and Bob managed the darkroom work after business hours. Now, years after we stopped the old-time portrait line, visitors still stick their head in the door to inquire about it.

Needless to say, we didn't have duplicate darkroom equipment in those early years. Luckily, however, we had a Suburban, so each year in late spring we dismantled the St. Louis darkroom, transported it to Colorado and set up business in Lake City.

All this was tantalizing Bob mercilessly. He was marking off the days until he could retire, run his photo business and live here full time. I was less miserable than he was. In fact, I was hardly miserable at all, but I could easily space out thinking about a new life in Colorado. I was on the faculty at Webster University in St. Louis, and I was being tapped more and more for administrative duties. The handwriting was on the wall - without a fight, and perhaps even with one, my future was not going to be filled with the free-spirited, creative days I'd known there for many years. I'd always worked hard long hours, but committee tasks were edging out class planning, and catalog compilation and editing weren't quite the same as writing a poem or preparing a Readers Theatre program. Most threatening of all was the possibility that I couldn't forever count on summers off to come to Colorado. On balance, though, my life was all right and my job better than most.

Rightfully so, Bob took the earliest possible retirement and moved to Lake City in July of 1984. Today he teases me by saying that there was a "year or so" when he commuted to St. Louis. I didn't retire until June of 1987. You do the math. In Lake City, he jogged to the lake almost daily; he was elected to the town council; he trained and became an emergency medical technician; he served as a director on the Chamber of Commerce Board. In short, he was engaged in this community and spending more time in Colorado than St. Louis. Well, who could blame him?

In the fall of 1986, I took an earned sabbatical and spent it in Lake City. That did it. As soon as I returned for the spring semester, I resigned, effective June of 1987.

We came to Colorado for one set of reasons, but we've stayed for quite another. Of course the two overlap, but the statement is true. Compared with today's rapid pace and the plight of many caught in meaningless jobs, time-guzzling commutes and urban pollution, our "trap" was minimal. Nevertheless, we were mesmerized by the thought of living in a quiet town surrounded by mountains, lakes, streams and wildflowers. Walking out our door to some of the most untouched areas in the country, skiing up a canyon only a few blocks from our house, living more quietly and simply - all seemed within our reach.

The 1970s were a time of shedding pretenses, others' social expectations and even material possessions. To be sure, we were influenced by that desire to "chuck it all and live the good life."

Only we didn't have a clue what the good life really was. While we still gasp in wonder at living in a place this beautiful, while we still hike and ski and fish and savor cookouts on the lake, only after becoming emotionally integrated into this small community did we realize what the good life is all about.

And Thirty Years Later

Here we are in the twenty-first century, some fifteen years since I started recording my life in a small mountain community, but some thirty years since I first laid eyes on Lake City. This is truly a different time; Lake City is a different place, and I see it through different eyes. Sometimes I strain hard to use those old eyes, to recapture that sensitivity to each of nature's nuances. Once in a while, I still have to catch my breath at seeing a deep purple sky or fresh snow glistening on spruce boughs. I still experience that overwhelming sense of satisfaction that says, sometimes subliminally, sometimes out loud, "This is my home. I really live in this beautiful place."

I used to chuckle when the "old timers" talked about the gruesome trip to Gunnison, sixty miles over a gravel, mud-rutted road, or how fierce the winters used to be. Now I guess I'm one of those old timers. Granted, several residents here go back much further than I, but a lot has happened in thirty years. Let me hasten to say that Lake City is still a very small place, so small in fact that I have learned to keep quiet about it more often than not.

"Oh, you live in the mountains?" a city resident somewhere remarks, no doubt envisioning a posh development outside Denver.

"Yes," I remark and take a sip of my wine. Below a certain population, "small" is something you can't explain. The 2000 census returns list the town residents at 373. Hinsdale County, once the most sparsely populated county in the country, now claims a whopping 790 souls. Lake City is the not only the county seat, it is the only town in Hinsdale County.

The Lake City I first met was considerably wilder and cruder than the community we know today. You can't picture a place more typically "Old West" than the Elkhorn Bar whose smell of stale beer and tobacco and the blast of jukebox country music jumped out at you a block away. Today the bank president sits at her computer at the very spot where the guys tucked their spurs up to the bar. Well, the Pine Cone, a close-by bar, might rival the Elkhorn. The Pine Cone has been skillfully renovated into a quality version of a nineteenth century saloon, renamed of course, and owned by a young couple from Chicago.

Our first summer here, we rounded up the kids, camp dirt and all, and went to Theresa's Place, a cafe on the historic strip of Silver Street where we watched an Outward Bound movie - the weekly entertainment. Today's visitors enjoy almost-first-run movies two or three nights a week in the Mountaineer Theatre. It's unique and rustic and the projector occasionally breaks down, provoking loud calls and whistles from the fifty or so viewers, but it's a movie house, nevertheless.

In the early 1990s I was instrumental in forming a local arts council and today its calendar lists some twenty different events from May to September - bands from Denver; plays; arts and crafts festivals; local musical productions. In the winter, town residents gather for local plays and talent shows.

Thirty years ago, we'd never heard of 911, but the phone number of a local nurse was posted here and there in case of an emergency. While the nearest hospital is still sixty miles away, a nurse practitioner staffs the Lake City Area Medical Center, and a well-trained and responsive corps of volunteer emergency medical technicians is a radio call away. The volunteer fire department has a new home, new trucks and a rigorous training program.

In our early years here, cowboys (or men dressed like them) tied horses to trees outside the Silver Street Saloon. It's now the Pueblo House gift shop.

Bob and I remember when workmen were digging out the Hole in the Wall, which became a popular basement-level saloon for many years but is now used by the local community theatre group, The Cabin Fever Players, for a green room and costume and prop storage. Remodeled into a theatre in the 1970s, the Black Crooke, above the Hole in the Wall, was heated until a very few years ago by an old barrel wood stove, and two cords of wood graced the south wall each winter. I know. I've helped stack it.

The Hole in the Wall was only one of the dreams of John and Ann Parker who bought several buildings in town in the 1970s. Where Stella Pavich once sat, regally made-up and coifed, behind a massive brass cash register awaiting sparse customers in "Mike's" grocery store, they created the elegant Mountain Harvest Restaurant. Today it is Mammy's Kitchen and Whiskey Bar, named after Stella, who recently died in a Gunnison nursing home. In the early '70s, we were amused at the vast, almost-vacant shelves spanning the room displaying their occasional can of green beans or loaf of bread while Stella played her role as proudly as if she were a queen overseeing a palace.

For several years, we dialed only the last four numbers for local calls. Come to think of it, the first couple of years we were in business, we didn't even have a phone. Street signs and house numbers came much later, and if memory serves me right, only one large luxurious second home dotted the mountainside.

I'm not complaining about the changes. I'm constantly grateful for the warm, creative, resourceful people who are choosing to make Lake City home. I had an early dream of starting a community theatre group here, but one day I stopped dreaming and did a reality check. I could count on one hand the number of people who might participate. Now the Cabin Fever Players has a mailing list of sixty people and considerable depth in casting shows.

Lake City has evolved from what seemed to be an ad hoc group of people and practices to a place with some highly effective systems. For the year 2000, the Lake City Arts Council received the Governor's Award for Excellence in the Arts.

We have indeed witnessed the "gentling" of Lake City - hopefully not the gentrification. So far, and we hope, forever, its gentler ways spring from the same heart.

A New Nest

 I have finally moved to Lake City, lock, stock and typewriter. I'm afraid the latter is not getting much use. I'm being held hostage by an army of cardboard boxes. I couldn't possibly write.

Of course, the clutter of boxes doesn't help, but I'm beginning to feel constricted in these close quarters attached to Silver Scene. Our one bedroom loft, our tiny living area with the loft stairs right in its middle, our improvised kitchen (we couldn't find room in the plans for all the appliances, so we left out the stove) were fine for summer stays. During those brief weeks, we'd been too busy running the business and hiking the trails to need a kitchen range or to think much about our living conditions. We knew, of course, that we'd have to move or add on once we really lived here.

Well, we really live here now, and I'm feeling cramped and unsettled, stumbling around cardboard boxes and thinking constantly about my friends in St. Louis, and former students and colleagues. We've spent years fitting the pieces, bit by bit, into the puzzle called "How to Live in Lake City," and now that I'm here my mind keeps straying a thousand miles east.

Perhaps if I think hard enough, I can conjure up some advantages to being back there.

For starters, back there I didn't have to worry about too much sunshine. We could go for days with hardly a glimmer. Just safe, grey skies. Here I watch that dangerous sunlight creep down the mountainside each morning, gradually bathing the valley with its magical warmth. Back there I never had to worry about sunlight so pleasant that I could run around in a sweatshirt in the winter. Or the way it turns roadside snow into banks of gems and warms the highway daily so that I can enjoy a lovely wintry world and dry pavement at the same time.

Furthermore, I was never in great danger of hitting deer on the city streets. I didn't need the keen, deer-scanning sight one develops up here. I never looked for tracks in the snow or strained to discern deer as they blended perfectly with winter's brown and white landscape. I don't recall ever watching them bounce along the road, spring over a fence and dissolve into the dusk. I never needed that special peripheral vision back there, except possibly for sighting speeding taxis approaching from side streets.

I was also perfectly safe from aspen trees. Granted, they are not generally dangerous except when I'm on cross-country skis, going downhill toward a curve in the trail. I've hugged a lot of trees lately. The city golf courses, the main place I skied back there are totally free of aspen trees. Since I didn't have to worry about slamming into them, neither did I see their charcoal shadows streaking across the snow, or the cream-colored, black-eyed trunks against the stark white floor of the woods.

Cows were never a problem either. Up here, you never know when you might run into a herd being driven somewhere as I did the other morning. I stopped the car and enjoyed watching them file orderly on either side. For a while. Then I noticed that they began to hesitate, bunch up at my front bumper and then nudge each other and crowd closer. I couldn't help wondering if I was in a stampede-about-to-happen over my car. In time, they unknotted themselves and moved on. Whatever I encountered back there, I was safe from cattle drives on my way to work.

I was in no danger of driving into the lake each morning because of some startling new lighting. Since I never drove around a lake at all, I wasn't distracted when it became a sea of dazzling diamonds. Or a blanket of variegated green and silver. Or a velvet white expanse.

I feel better now. I know I made the right move, but why can't I escape those boxes? Why do I unpack, pack, sort and rearrange all that stuff? Why can't I get on with my new life and sit down and write about this glorious place? Why is there always one more errand to run, meal to plan, phone call to make, closet to straighten? Or one more box to unpack? I know that chores don't stay done and that we make our own choices about what can wait and what cannot.

I'm trying to quit beating up on myself and realize that some very big things have been happening in my life: I have ended a twenty year career in higher education, sold a home of twenty-four years, moved from a city where our children were born and raised, left close friends with whom we've shared many milestones. Perhaps more overwhelming than all of that, however, is that I'm experiencing the culmination of our long-range plan. I am living a dream come true. We don't often expect dreams to come true, so when they do, we don't quite know how to behave.

No wonder I feel strange. These boxes link my past and my future. From their contents I am making a new nest.

It's been a long time coming.

Colorado Fall

 I had promised myself that I would not write about the fall colors. Some things, after all, are better left to the painter and photographer. However, this is my first Colorado fall, and I'll take my chances on being trite because there is no way I'm going to keep quiet about it.

For years, I've heard local residents praise September. They describe calm, dry, sunny days with a backdrop of splendid fall colors. At last, this year I didn't have to head east in mid-August. Finally, I have experienced a San Juan September.

On the first day of September, I looked outside. The surrounding peaks were covered with snow. The next few days were cool and rainy with a little sleet thrown in for bad measure. I was convinced that winter was here and that the proverbial September had been a collective hallucination. Then suddenly one morning, the legendary September burst into life.

It was chock full of surprises. I don't know how I thought the color change would happen, but I was surprised at the aspen's gradual paling to a lighter green. Such a subtle prelude marked by an occasional startling dash of yellow.

I had been told that aspen groves would look like honey flowing down the mountain. They didn't tell me about the breathtaking strands of red and variegated orange. Who would have thought that the common cottonwood would join in the act? Or that ordinary bushes would splash the roadside with yellow as if to say, "Me too! Me too!" I was not prepared for the medley of ground foliage - yellow, red, persimmon, forming graceful patterns on slopes and bluffs. How surprising was a hillside sparkling with inches-high aspen.

How unexpected were tiny yellow leaves spattering on the windshield like summer bugs. Who would have pictured the wind whisking golden aspen leaves into the arms of spruce, decorating them like Christmas trees? Nobody could possibly have prepared me for what sunlight does to all that color.

For our mutual safety, we should institute a designated driver program for the color season. You cannot safely operate a motorized vehicle and watch this fall spectacle at the same time. On a recent drive, with someone else at the wheel, the images continued to bombard me: trees literally glow when backlit by the evening sun. Ordinary brown roads and ditches don golden carpets. A single aspen stand displays several colors at once— shades of deep green, lime, chartreuse and pure yellow. Some yellow trees are persimmon-shaded only at the top. Occasionally, one flaming aspen presses against a deep green backdrop, and occasionally, one somber evergreen presses against a flaming yellow backdrop. Slender ribbons of color trail delicately down ravines. In quiet places, the streams turn golden.

There's enough splendor to cause any remotely sensitive driver to topple off a cliff. If you can't find a designated driver, go slowly and stop often. Be forewarned. Driving in Colorado in September can be hazardous to your health.

In the midst of this blazing gold, we decided to go camping. Our campsite was tucked under a cliff on the east side by a stream. We awakened to a biting-cold morning in a frosty tent. At breakfast, a plastic juice container sailed smoothly down the length of the icy picnic table. I cooked with metal pots numbing my fingers while the coffee in my cup cooled in midair.

Aside from fall's blazing spectacle, I've been most surprised by its capriciousness. On the afternoon before this freezing morning, we had hiked in shorts, retrieved the buried sunscreen from the bottom of the pack and welcomed a shady spot for lunch. The distant peaks were white.

When I was growing up in Missouri, September was a definite month. Completely predictable. We took lazy walks home from school, tentatively testing new friendships. We sat in sultry evenings on porch steps, happily squandering some time between summer and the school year's full momentum. We wore new sweaters to school long before it was cold enough, and new shoes that had to be that year's style, but not look too new.

One September my friends startled me with a surprise hayride birthday party. Toward the end of the ride, we stretched out on backs on the sticky, warm hay to count stars and trace constellations. Later one friend's mother scolded us harshly - all those prone bodies of mixed sexes. So much for September in the Midwest in the fifties.

The first day of school was always hot and memorable. I can still smell my new yellow box of eight pointed Crayola crayons. When my own children were young, September was the ritual trip to the shopping center to purchase items on the required school supply list. Through their lists, some teachers communicated their style in no uncertain terms. Those shopping trips were filled with tension and fear that we might purchase the wrong style folder. Other trips were filled with excitement over what might happen with all those neat supplies. The Crayola boxes had grown from eight to sixty-four, which I thought was magnificent for one generation's progress, but which didn't particularly impress my children. Those predictable Septembers were precious. How different from these playful, fickle mountain falls.

With September's passing, the yellow splendor has faded, fallen and mostly flown away. Aspen and cottonwood look dull and naked, stretching their bony fingers skyward. Tourist crowds have long since gone, and we wonder, "Could we possibly be missing them already?" The hunters are here, dotting the town with orange, but they're a purposeful lot, not much inclined to amble around, looking things over. Who got their elk, and where is the local news of the day? A certain restlessness has set in. I suspect that it conceals an unspoken half-wish that the snow would come. No one dares voice it, however, knowing that it will come, perhaps too often, too deep and for too long.

A popular metaphor refers to fall as middle age with allusions to the endings of things. Up here, fall is pure adolescence, not knowing what it is or what it wants to be. On a drive through September's colors, it teases us with patches of leftover green. With that summer green at our sides, we look straight ahead at golden groves pressed against white mountains. Like a spirited adolescent, one minute it is placid, at peace with itself, and the next it is hurling aspen leaves like snow. Then to prove its confusion, it hurls snow itself. Like the adolescent's parent, at times we wish it would settle down and grow up. But, of course, we sure hate to see it go.

You Stay Up Here All Winter?

After several years of being in business here and meeting tourists from lots of different places, I can safely claim that the question most asked by summer visitors is, "Do you stay up here all winter?" I understand the fascination. In the years that we came to Lake City in the summers only, I was intrigued by what winter must be like. Packing for camping in the mountains - mittens, hats and down gear - on steamy, 90 plus degree St. Louis days, I reasoned, "If Lake City can get this cold in August, what must the winters be like?" Flawed logic to be sure.

My first urge when answering that perpetual question is to reply that having lived in northern Maine for two years I know what winter is and that Colorado winters are a piece of cake.

Bob was a pilot in the Air Force when we were married, and our first two years together were spent in Maine, not far from the Canadian border. We moved there in the fall of 1954 with a little reprieve before the snow started. It began one November Sunday; I distinctly remember crossing the street to church in my high-heeled pumps. By the time we came out of the service, I was wading snow up to my ankles. The next day I went in search of galoshes – boots were not in our vocabulary in the fifties – and little did I realize that my feet would be wedded to them until May.

Our first winter there broke records for both amount of snowfall and low temperatures. Bob called me once while on a plane-ferrying trip to Arizona and told me that it was seventy-six degrees. The night before, our temperature had dipped to fifty-five below zero.

Base housing had not been immediately available when we moved to Maine, so we rented part of an old house in town. Today it would be called a townhouse, but that wasn't in our 1950s vocabulary, either. Our part consisted of a small living room and kitchen downstairs, and two bedrooms and a bath upstairs. The house had no central heating of any kind. Our landlady was a classic Maine native. "If it gets really cold, you can plug in the heater in the bathroom," she assured us.

"Really cold" meant when the ice formed on the inside walls of the stairway. As newlyweds, we'd race each other up the cold stairs and jump under the mountainous pile of covers and watch our breath puff white around us as we talked. Later we discovered that our ill-heated house in town was a blessing in disguise. The base houses had been designed for somewhere in Florida, and through some government snafu, they had ended up in northern Maine. Looking back, that was probably an Air Force rumor, but we did know from friends' experiences that the housing's insulation and heating didn't work well in Maine winters.

Our house had a detached garage set some fifty feet from the street. As the snows started, Bob's parents wrote that they were so pleased we had a garage to keep the car in. By the time the snows really showed us what they could do, we were lucky to shovel a car's length into the driveway. For a young man, Bob was extremely committed to our survival. He'd shovel his way out of the driveway in the morning as he went to the base; he'd shovel his way in at lunchtime, and invariably the city snowplows would bury the driveway while he was having lunch, and he'd shovel his way out again.

We discovered that a cigarette lighter was a valuable tool for thawing our car locks so we could get in, and that a razor blade was essential for scraping the ice off the inside of our windshield. We learned that getting up in the middle of the night to run the car's engine was the best insurance that it would start in the morning. We found out what it was like to look up to the tops of snow tunnels to our front door and what 3:00 p.m. darkness feels like.

Driving to Maine the first time, we heard on the radio obituaries that "interment" would be in the spring. To a couple of Missourians, that made no sense. Nor did the clotheslines on the front porches. We didn't have to endure a Maine winter for long to realize that you don't bury people in frozen ground nor do you hang clothes in your backyard.

So, spending the winters up here isn't nearly the challenge that most Texans perceive it to be. Nevertheless, there were adjustments. For starters, I had to separate the idea of cold and snow from the idea of winter. In the Midwest, even in Maine, snow and cold come in winter. Up here, they can come anytime – July and August are both fine candidates. The main difference is that the summer storms are short-lived, and literally in minutes, the weather switches seasons.

The second lesson I had to learn is that winter up here is a teaser. As a rule, our autumns are long and balmy. To be sure, the wildflowers fade; the aspen gold blows away or falls under foot to be trampled into brown. The peaks turn white, and early mornings, a scrim of ice edges the lake. Night temperatures plunge to winter-like numbers, and frost finally claims the petunia beds.

However, each morning, the sun inches down the mountain to warm the town, and the pleasant afternoons are clear and gorgeous. All around town people ask "How much longer can this go on?" We hear the flurry of construction workers as they make the most of each warm day. Children play outside till dusk in shirtsleeves. Townspeople fight against inside chores, and plan yet one more outing to bask in the lovely days.

On such a day, a friend and I decided to attempt one more hike in the high country. We drove some ten miles into the mountains, above Capitol City, and walked the road toward Engineer Pass. Though Capitol City has only one original building standing, the valley is so full of ghosts that it's not hard to imagine the old town teeming with 3,000 people during the height of mining days. Town leaders fully believed that it would one day be Colorado's capital.

Along the road, yesterday's golden stands had turned to grey fleece dotted with an occasional dull gold spot. Tenacious asters formed bunches of beige puff balls as perfectly arranged as they had been in their days of purple glory. The whole valley had become one huge, dried flower bouquet, a quiet epilogue to the exuberant fall. We walked in shirtsleeve weather in the sun, while in the shade, snow trimmed the trail, pebbles dappled the snow, and blue ice circled stones across puddles.

Our destination was a little log cabin at the base of the Engineer Pass road. Dating back to the prospecting days, I'm sure, the cabin has been used in subsequent years by sheepherders and finally became a beloved landmark for hikers and jeepers. We'd picnicked there on many shimmering July days, in drizzle on blustery August afternoons, in awesome thunderstorms. We crossed the creek on ice-ringed stones and tromped through knee-deep snow where we thought the path to the cabin should be. In summer, the cabin sits in a field of wildflowers, flanked by a stream and waterfall, almost too picturesque to be believed. Now it sat in glistening snow, broken only by busy animal tracks.

The sun had melted an ideal picnic spot between two tall pines. We spread the poncho tablecloth. Raingear is surplus on such a day, but conditioned by summer's whims, I'd left it in the pack. We ate our lunch in this sunlit spot on a day as glorious as any that summer could offer.

So I've learned that winter up here pays no attention to the calendar. It's not unlike waiting to go into labor. You know for sure it's coming; you're just not sure when. On the one hand, you want it to happen soon; on the other hand, you still have lots to do before the event. You'll love it when it gets here, but you also know it will take up your time and be a heap of trouble. It will be beautiful, but you'll wistfully recall how simple life was before it came. Maybe seasonal-limbo isn't such a bad state after all.

With the awareness that the extended, warm fall cannot last forever comes a sort of dread of the first snow. Emily Dickinson wrote, "I dreaded that first robin so." A peculiar sentiment, but I think I've shared a sense of it, though there is nothing final about the first snowfall. Normally, the first snow is short-lived with many more pleasant sunny days skipping at its heels before the snow settles in for the season. But emotionally, it's symbolic – not so much the beginning of a season as the end of one.

Almost without exception, the first real snow comes on a day when I have to travel. I squint sullenly, offering no welcome to the swirling white streaks parting in front of my windshield. Then winter

starts its eternal wooing. Like responding to the slow warming after a lovers' quarrel, I give in and acknowledge the beauty the storm has wrought. How could I have forgotten those massive dark pines draped with heavy white scallops? The startling contrast of the shady river, still bustling, with the snow-filled cottonwood arms arching over it? Thick snow almost closes the gaps between aspen limbs, creating shapes like giant paper cutouts against canyon walls. Fleece trims every roadside bush, every weed. Low, misty clouds cling around peaks in ragged swatches. Inevitably, the triumphant sun begins its morning play.

After that hasty preview, the next snow will seem more mature, seasoned, like the real thing. The kind that takes its time, shifting lazily downward with occasional horizontal detours, taking hours to dust a pine tree, even longer to cling to bare aspen boughs. It bunches in little cotton-balls on the cinquefoil bush that still wears springs of dried blooms. Like Dickinson said of her robin "But he is mastered now," I'll be all right now. The snow begins to feel like a familiar visitor returned.

I recall one first real snow that started on a Saturday night. On Sunday morning, our town was nestled inside a cocoon of gray and white. No Round Mountain overlooked the town on the south; no Station Eleven towered over it on the east, not even a peak to the north. What little world was visible was draped in strange shapes. Cars had become white mounds; wheelbarrows bore new cargo. I have never experienced quiet like a Lake City Sunday morning after a snowfall. Everyone seemed to have taken a silent oath to preserve the peace for as long as possible. Even the dogs had hidden out somewhere. First snowfalls in St. Louis were hyper affairs, frantic assaults with blowers and shovels, all to the high-pitched background squeal of spinning tires – all-out warfare. Here, when the town finally began to stir, it moved in slow motion. The seasoned wisdom prevailed, "You might as well wait awhile and let the sun do a lot of the work." Besides, we can walk wherever we want to go anyway.

On that first walk in the real snow, I felt as if I were meeting old friends. The pines, heavy with white, frosted the mountainside and pressed against blue sky. A lone jay hopped tentatively in the snowy limbs of a cottonwood. Fence posts sported those funny pointed hats. The white popped the colors out. Even the pastel houses seemed brighter. It was hard to believe that just yesterday the crunchy sound under my feet was dried leaves.

One of my most vivid memories of winter up here is my first Lake City Christmas. I knew about big-city malls, sophisticated holiday parties, seasonal symphony and theatre events, to say nothing of office celebrations. But I didn't know about a Lake City Christmas.

First of all, there was the setting. The white town sparkled under moon and streetlight glow. Dapple that with reflections of colored lights and you have a storybook winter village.

No shopping center décor could rival Tub Carl's annual ice sculpture on the banks of the Lake Fork of the Gunnison River. I was out walking on a sunny afternoon when suddenly before me towered a marvelous coke-bottle green, free-form ice sculpture. I literally gasped at the unexpected beauty. I suppose if you live in the midst of striking beauty all the time, you may be more inclined to create it.

An ice sculpture formed by a dripping hose turned on a tree or other structure may be a simple idea, but on the banks of the Lake Fork of the Gunnison, the sculpture seemed a perfect metaphor. If you know the temperature will be below freezing, don't fight it, use it.

In this greeting-card setting, the community holiday season started with the school play in the Black Crooke Theatre in the heart of downtown. The stage set, decorations and costumes, as well as the performance, represented weeks of work and energy. More important than the product, however, was the wave of support and love, almost visible, that welled from the audience. The kids felt as if they were on Broadway. That was the community's gift to them. At the end of the school performance, audience members were reminded to carry their folding chairs back across the street to the armory where a potluck that my city friends wouldn't believe followed.

A few nights later, the community choir gave us "A Gift in Song," a delightful program of varied seasonal music. How can so much talent be concentrated in this small place?

The annual potluck and party at the Presbyterian Church offered a spontaneous program that ranged from renditions of hackneyed holiday poems to old-timers telling stories of Christmas past.

You haven't been Christmas caroling until you've huddled on a flatbed trailer with thirty or more people being inched around town by horses under a dazzling winter sky, filling the air with the sounds of Christmas.

Almost anyone who has vacationed here remembers the summer steak fry events up the jeep road to the top of Vickers' Mountain overlooking Lake San Cristobal. Try it by snowmobile on Christmas Eve. To be honest, it started snowing pretty hard by the time we had all the meat on the grill. Our plastic knives broke in the cold, and grease formed on the steaks. We had great fun anyway.

Fill in the odd moments with private gatherings, snowmobiling to the top of the world, cross-country skiing through silent aspen groves or snuggling by a crackling fire to enjoy the view outside. Families clustered; friends became family; acquaintances became friends. There seemed to be room in the inn for all.

The holiday visitors leave. One by one, the lights are unstrung. Abandoned skeletal Christmas trees rest at odd angles in the snowbanks, their bony fingers pointing skyward. Bowls of leftover candy gather dust on counters. A stray sprig of red garland glitters as it cartwheels in the snow. Another shop closes. Business hours are once again revised and posted.

Real winter is here. Over the years, I have discovered what real winter means. First of all, it's when you look up and discover that there aren't many of you left in town. It's when you wake up to some pretty scary figures on the thermometer. Thirty -two below zero is the low in my experience.

In real winter I've learned to pack my freezer full of casseroles and my imagination full of recipes because we won't dash out for fast food (or even slow food) just any old time I don't feel like cooking. Real winter is when you drive sixty miles to see a movie and hope you time the trip between storms.

Real winter is when you eye the shrinking woodpile and calculate, figure and hope. Winter is when you're thankful for little things: your car starting, your pipes flowing, your flue drawing and your boots repelling. Real winter is when you find yourself not only staring at a strange car in town, but talking about it as well.

Winter is a time when we are immersed in constant vivid beauty. We're assured of seeing deer and elk grazing like cattle. If we're lucky, we may come upon the whole herd at dusk, thundering toward higher ground, flinging clouds of snow in their wake. Surrounded by a universe of glistening white, intense blue skies and shimmering sunny days, I've pinched myself and asked, "Can this really be my own vast playground?"

Real winter is when you come to terms with why you're here, when you learn what community really means. It's a time for spontaneous get-togethers and homemade entertainment. Contrary to what people must think, we sometimes create too much to do. Yet if one can make the hard choices, winter can become a reprieve from everything, a time for reflection and renewal, a delightful interlude in which one can easily believe that there is plenty of time.

Obviously, my blatant bias is that Lake City winters are a well-kept secret. I have fun with that perpetual question, "You really stay up here all winter?"

Visitor: I guess you're pretty well snowed in up here in winter?

Me: Well, actually, we're almost never snowed in. The school bus takes our junior high and high schoolers to Gunnison daily. Actually, our kids missed more school in St. Louis because of weather than the kids do here.

Visitor: Is that right? But, of course, the other road - Slumgullion Pass - it wouldn't be open.

Me: Well, actually, Slum is not only open, it's surprisingly clear. We go up there to ski quite a bit. There may be packed snow and icy patches on sheltered stretches, but there's a lot of clear, dry pavement as well.

Visitor: No kidding! How much snow do you get up here?

Me: Well, actually, more than Houston and less than Crested Butte.

Visitor: Seriously, now.

Me: Well, actually, that's a hard question to answer. Depends on the year. Last year it snowed on seven days in December, accumulating twenty-one and a half inches. Eighteen days in December, incidentally, were clear or mostly clear. January had only five snow days for a total of seven inches. February, six days of snow with traces on five others. Now get this, March is supposed to be our snowiest month, but this year we had only three days of snow for a total of three and a half inches!

Visitor: Well, I'll be. Hmm. Gets pretty cold, though, huh?

Me: Well actually, that's not easy to answer. One answer is, "You bet."It can get thirty below at night. Keep in mind that we're hardly ever running around outside in the middle of the night. In the daytime, we are outside running around, often in a sweatshirt or even shirtsleeves. On calm sunny days, and we have a lot of them, you wouldn't believe the actual temperatures.

Visitor: Golleee. How many of you stay up here anyway?

Me: Actually, fewer than 300.

Visitor: What in the world do you do up here all winter?

Me: How long do you have?

Visitor: Ha! I sure would like to see it in the winter.

Me: Well, come on up. Believe me, we'll be real happy to see you.

One sunny December afternoon, Bob and I drove into and beyond Sherman town site, a ghost town that had been washed away by floods on more than one occasion during the mining days. Picturesque Cottonwood Creek, the site of summer picnics and Sunday outings, was almost completely frozen over. It glistened with swirls of white and shiny pale green ice.

We got out of the car for a closer look. Pausing for a moment at the log bridge to the Cataract Falls Trail, I sensed, more than saw, a movement a bit upstream. I ducked a few yards through the low trees to the next clearing by the stream. Form, rather than movement caught my eye: a fat beaver, balanced on his paddle tail, looked at me and I at him.

He was sitting on the icy streambed near the lone spot of open water. I froze, expecting him to make his smacking, splashing exit into the water. Instead, he lifted his chin a bit, apparently assessing this strange odor, and continued to stare. After a few moments, he eased down on all fours and slowly plodded toward the opposite shore. I held my breath as I realized that I might be about to observe him in action.

The beaver reached the other shore, waddled a foot or so onto the bank, and in what seemed like seconds, felled a small aspen. With the trunk clinched in his mouth, he dragged the tree, branches trailing, across the ice to the open spot of water. Suddenly he dove. As he tugged from under the surface, the limbs slid into the water like trailing fingers of a sinking swimmer. Anchoring the tree to the bottom of the stream, he was assembling his winter food supply.

Abruptly he surfaced. His slick wet coat was shiny ebony. Resting on his tail and back legs, he vigorously rubbed his face and ears with two front paws. In an instant, his fur fluffed and bronzed. Off he trudged to the far shore. This time he seemed to do absolutely nothing there, returned to the water, dove quietly again, emerged, ruffled his face and ears, and headed for the bank again.

On some trips, he brought back small trees or branches; on others, I could determine no purpose whatsoever for his journey. Busy as a beaver he certainly was, but I was beginning to wonder how he'd score on a time and motion study.

We watched for about an hour. Each time he moved to the opposite shore, we'd inch closer to the water. Finally we were standing at the stream's edge, no more than ten feet from his open water spot. He seemed not remotely interested in our presence. The sun slipped behind the mountain and became a bright cold twilight at two p.m.

As we left, I snapped a small branch under my foot. The beaver slapped his tail with a thunderous crack, the only sign of alarm he'd sounded during our visit.

Why was he working out there alone in broad daylight? On a Sunday, too. Didn't he know that all self-respecting beavers secure their winter's food in the fall? Any normal December that diving hole would be ice-capped.

I can only surmise that he, like us, was trying to make the most of a mixed up, delayed season.

Once the new year progresses far enough along that our individual resolutions are seriously battered if not broken, I think we should make some as a community.

We should definitely resolve not to tell anyone that our thermometer touched eighteen below zero when the nation's coldest temperature was reported at minus eleven. On second thought, perhaps we should consider the proposal of the local hairdesser. He claims, in response to the population influx, that it's time to abandon our "beautiful winter" stories and revert to our "Thirty below, cloudy, windy, buried-in-snow" script.

We do need a resolution about rumors. Let's resolve that we won't pass on a rumor unless it has been verified by at least three other people. Of course, in order to authenticate it, we'll have to stop the first three people we meet and ask, "Say, did you hear about....?"

To ensure our collective efficiency and guarantee productive use of our time, we should resolve to limit midday errands to no more than one and one-half hours. Allowing a maximum of two minutes driving time, we are still left with approximately eighty-six minutes to spend as we wish among the bank, post office, grocery store and filling stations. This should be sufficient for average erran needs. On special occasions, when we have additional stops, we can trim it off our travel time.

Speaking of errand interactions, we need to resolve to limit the amount of time spent in car-to-car conversations to ten minutes. Unless, of course, the dialogue is taking place on a street with sufficient shoulder space for approaching vehicles to pull around. In such cases, let's stick to the old rules and talk all day if we're so inclined. However, under no circumstances can a third party engage in the conversation and thereby block the shoulder detour. Well, possibly under special conditions, depending on the topic, a third party could participate, but four conversants, resulting in the blocking of both shoulders, must be prohibited.

On second thought, let's shelve that productive-use-of-time idea. What we need is to spend more time in whimsical interactions. I gleefully killed a good hour once talking with a neighbor about his theory of the conspiracy that the local crows are clearly involved in. Wouldn't it be fun, just once, to tell a winter tourist, "Sure you can get to Ouray over the pass just like your map says."

Furthermore, we resolve that everyone in town will order firewood by April 1.

And, of course, we must do something about the loose dogs.

Enough of this frivolous stuff. What we really need to resolve is that we won't have a major fight this winter. Granted, there are several issues bubbling under the surface that could erupt into the winter volcano, but wouldn't it be interesting to spend a winter without the explosion? Well, maybe not as interesting, but probably healthier.

Looking ahead to next summer, all of us, particularly business owners, should resolve always to smile and chat with visitors, even when we're telling the two hundredth person that day, "Yes, indeed. We really do spend the winters here."

Although, "You stay up here all winter?" is no doubt the most frequently asked question, the most amusing is "What do you do up here all winter?"

"Very little of what I'd planned" is probably the best answer.

Once in a great while, an evening comes along when there's no meeting, no deadline, no party and nothing on television that anyone with a mental age over eight would watch. I cherish those rare nights when I can go browsing. I suppose it's a nerd's version of cruising or barhopping, but my idea of browsing is leafing through accumulated catalogs, catching up on magazine articles or exploring old books.

One such night, I ran across my dusty copy of *Walker's Rhyming Dictionary*. I realize that browsing in a rhyming dictionary wouldn't be everyone's idea of a hot time. For most people, it is about as useless as an outdoor pool in Lake City in January. I suppose that's why the editor's note struck me so funny. It seemed so incongruous. What I'd considered to be pure esoterica, a rhyming dictionary, turned out to have a pragmatic use.

John Walker originally published the rhyming dictionary in 1775. I'm not sure when my edition was published (I've had it at least forty years), but its print is tiny and ancient, with the text of each page boxed in a double-line border. The "Editor's Preface" is a leisurely *xlvi* pages, followed by an *xx* page introduction. If that tells you the flavor of the book, you will see why the editor's sales pitch jarred a bit.

The pitch is under the heading, Telegraphic Errors and it goes like this: "Among other uses of the Rhyming Dictionary, and one that will most commend it to commercial men, is the assistance it affords in deciphering errors in telegrams. All merchants having business relations with America or the Far East use Telegraph Codes..."

The words were often mutilated in transmission. Should the first part of the word be lost, as apparently was common, then *Walker's Rhyming Dictionary* could save the day. For example, a merchant receives a telegram that contains the word Sterturn which makes no sense at all. By the time the merchant returns the telegram to the company for a corrected message, the price of cotton has fallen and the merchant stands to lose a lot of money.

Had he owned *Walker's Rhyming Dictionary*, he could have checked it for all the words ending with *erturn*, found the word *overturn*, which would have made sense in the telegraphic context, and thereby saved hundreds of dollars.

The next time I'm totally disgusted by the barrage of television advertisement trying to sell me products I can't live without, I'll take pleasure in recalling that no one recently has tried to sell me *Walker's Rhyming Dictionary*.

With beavers to visit and books to browse, who said there's not much to do up here in winter?

Brenda Wagner, Lake City resident

A Foolproof Communication System

 I think the next Lake City visitors' guide should include under things-to-do "Be sure to visit the Lake City post office at noon." It's certainly one of my favorite things to do.

By contrast, where I used to live, going to the post office was among my least favorite things to do. To begin with, the parking lot accommodated about one-third of the customers who arrived at any given time, so the other two-thirds circled the area, honking and trying to bluff their way into the next available space. At the Lake City post office, you can take your time in the parking lot. You can leaf through your mail, carry on a car-to-car conversation or watch other people sitting in their cars reading their mail intently. In the parking lot, you may step over a dog sprawling patiently in the sun, or greet other dogs that poke their heads out of pickup beds to see what's up.

Once inside the post office where I used to live, you had to pull a paper number from the machine to determine your turn in line. Then blue-uniformed officials barked out the numbers while you stood tensed, ready to dash to the counter, like a runner waiting for the gun.

The Lake City post office is so user-friendly that you can forget your box key and still get your mail and a smile as well. You can forget your wallet and still mail your package. You can drop your Out of Town mail in the Local slot or vice-versa, and nobody gets upset.

At the post office where I used to live, you stood in lots of lines with your paper number in hand. There aren't many lines in Lake City. There are, however, small clusters of people, and they often group in front of your post office box. Key leading, you learn to do a stretch and balance act and reach around them. If your box is near the floor, you can squat and say, "Excuse me," and the cluster will usually shift a bit. If not, it doesn't matter because you're not in much of a rush and chances are you'll join the cluster before long anyway.

With the traffic, parking crunch and lines, a trip to the post office where I used to live could consume a considerable amount of time. Up here, a trip to the post office also takes a chunk out of the day, but for entirely different reasons. At most, it's a two-minute drive for almost everybody, but a round trip can easily take forty-five minutes. It's probably a rumor, but I've heard the record is held by a woman who arrived at the post office at noon. Her family called Search and Rescue around dark. If I were ever inclined to commit a local crime, I'd plan it around noon because nobody's minding any store.

The Lake City post office is the most foolproof of all the informal communication systems going here. Where else would you find a bulletin board home for lost postcards? People gather to read the postcards-with-no-address but with personal messages for all to see:

Dear Mark,

It's beautiful, wish you were here. Bethany went jeeping with Roger. Kevin will be furious. Don't tell anyone.

Love,

Marita

It's at the post office that you hug visitors upon their arrival. And there that you wish them a safe trip home. The post office is where you learn about the birth of a baby, new jobs, illness, divorce and death. Funeral notices are taped on the glass doors so all will know.

I want Lake City to thrive in many ways, but I do hope that home mail delivery is a long way off.

Don't Sweat The String Beans

Recently, out of the blue, I remembered a small book of mine that I hadn't seen since the move to Lake City. I don't know how I could have missed it in unpacking the numerous cardboard boxes of books that I insisted on moving with me. It was, after all, a very special book, so important, in fact, that I've tried to make its lead essay, "Why I Never Bawl Out a Waitress," the philosophical moorings for my life. I knew the essence of the essay, but I wanted to read the actual words again. The book is a small paperback collection of short pieces by Harry Golden called *Only in America*.

To give you an idea of how far back this book and I go together, it originally cost me fifty cents, and the foreword was written by Carl Sandburg. I was given pause for thought when I realized that the book would be well over thirty years old and that I would not likely find it on the shelves of an ordinary bookstore. When The Tattered Cover in Denver didn't have it, I felt as if I'd lost an old friend.

Then miraculously, while looking through a box I was sure I had searched before, there it was! The edges were tawny, and brittle pages fell from its spine when I turned them, but I had found it, nevertheless.

The essay I cherish goes something like this: Golden says he never bawls out a waitress when he remembers that there are at least four billion suns in the Milky Way - which is only one galaxy. Many of these suns are thousands of times larger than ours and have whole planetary systems of their own, some with billions of satellites. And this is only the Milky Way, our own small galaxy. There are billions of galaxies, and the farther you go in space, the thicker they become. Our own sun and its planets, including Earth, are in one tiny corner of the universe.

"When you think of all this," Golden says, "it's silly to worry whether the waitress brought you string beans instead of limas."

I don't consider Golden's view as apathetic. It isn't that our little corner isn't important. Remembering this piece simply helps me line up the priorities a bit.

Up here, a lot of people seem to have that perspective. On the surface, the opposite may seem to be true. We become embroiled in our inflated issues and sometimes behave as if Lake City is the center of the galaxy, if not the universe.

However, watch us closely in a pinch - when something important needs to be done or when tragedy, loss or serious illness hit. Then you will see a group of seemingly disparate people pulling together - people who seem to have figured out what's important and try to live their lives accordingly.

When you've figured out what really matters in life, though it may be different from what your neighbor has concluded, you don't often get hung up on string beans.

When the chips are down, we have very few waitress bashers up here.

Grant Houston, editor, The Silver World

The Wrong People Are Seldom In The Store

Sometimes I wonder why I read the newspaper or watch the news on television. Both contain too many reminders of how cruel people can be to each other. About the time I find myself asking how human beings can do such things to other human beings, I fumble around for my rose-colored glasses and think about the almost daily reminders that people do still care for each other. Up here, at least, people still go out of their way to be helpful.

My experiences probably fall into the "Only in a Small Town" category, but I strongly suspect that big city residents could also tell these stories - they just might have to look a little harder.

Some time ago, I was managing a local ranch. At bill-paying time I was waiting for a check from the owner to deposit before mailing the outgoing bills. My plans were made to leave town on a trip, and still no check arrived. I mentioned my dilemma at the local bank. An employee replied, "No problem." Without hesitation, she offered to hold the stack of outgoing bills until the deposit was safely made, then personally mail them for me. Not only was I shocked, but I trusted the person to do exactly what she had promised.

Desperate for a certain weight raincoat before making another trip, I called a store in a neighboring town. The store had several in stock, so I planned to go by the store as I left on the trip. However, I discovered that the store would not be open on the day I would pass through the town.

"No problem," the clerk related. "I'll take the coats home with me and you can come by my house and try them on." This person had never met me; she was not the owner of the store, just a clerk, but one that no doubt had established a great deal of trust with her employer.

I had a several hundred-dollar printing job done in another neighboring town print shop. Once again, I discovered that the shop would not be open when I planned to pick up the job.

"No problem," the owner remarked. "I'll leave the front door open. Just turn the lock when you leave."

I asked a friend to accompany me to Gunnison for a short dental appointment, after which we could have lunch and do some shopping for an upcoming theatrical production. I dropped her off at a local store and assured her that I would pick her up out front within the hour. Unfortunately, I had been confused about the nature of the dental appointment. When over an hour passed, I explained to the dentist that I was becoming very uncomfortable about my friend waiting for me. I needed to call and see if I could locate her.

"We can do better than that," the dentist replied. "We'll go get her and bring her back here to wait."

I argued a bit that they had work to do, that they could at least use my car, but they were as insistent as if this were part of their daily services to patients. I called the local store to ask if someone could possibly go out front, locate my friend and explain that someone from the dentist's office would be picking her up. The woman who answered the phone didn't even hesitate.

Another friend stopped by a Gunnison store before it opened one morning, but the clerk saw her waiting and invited her in anyway. My friend was looking for a particular booklet, and the clerk was apologetic that they had apparently sold out of it.

"Oh, I know what!" she exclaimed. "I have one at home. If you'll watch the store for a few minutes, I'll run home and get it." And she did.

The same friend placed her purse in her basket while shopping at a local store and strayed away to examine some merchandise. Item by item, she filled another basket and later approached the checkout counter. Only then did she realize that she'd been loading someone else's basket and that she had no idea where her purse might be. She hurried back to the aisle where she'd parked her first cart, already planning her strategy for notifying credit card companies and other appropriate authorities that her purse had been stolen. The cart sat where she'd left it, moved not an inch, with purse, cards and cash intact.

As a victim of several thefts in cities over the years, I certainly don't recommend leaving one's purse in a shopping cart. Granted, the wrong people weren't in the store that day.

The more I've thought about it, the more it seems to me that up here the right people are always around.

It's A Lot Like Spring Only Something's Wrong

When asked what being old is like, an elderly man replied, "Well, it's exactly like being young, except something's wrong."

That pretty well pegs the way I feel about this season that follows winter up here. It's a lot like spring, only something's wrong. What's wrong is that no forsythia bushes are flashing in the morning sunlight, no jonquils are pushing green spears through black soil, no hyacinths are perfuming moist air, no green is spreading across lawns, no redbuds are budding. What's wrong is that in most parts of the country, people are gathering tulip bouquets while we're counting the sticks in the last stack of firewood. Back in St. Louis, March's forsythia splashed yellow across greening suburban lawns; April exploded in a parade of redbud, flowering crab and azalea, and by May, spring was a settled resident hosting the late-leafing oak and a few hot days.

So here I am, thinking about that season I love so much, looking at a thermometer showing a single-digit temperature and watching winds scatter torn trash bags released by melting snow. How paradoxical that in the mountains where the climate is so dramatic, spring is an understatement. In other places, where the climate is generally a bore, spring erupts with colors so vibrant that you can almost hear the outburst. I have come to the conclusion that "Springtime in the Rockies" is an oxymoron.

After a couple of "springs" through which I grumbled constantly, I decided to make my peace with the season by running away to visit places where spring happens the way it's supposed to. One year we took a long car trip specifically designed to take us through several springs. In late March, we headed south. We knew we were out of the mountain winter when an official rest stop sign in New Mexico read "Watch for Rattlesnakes." In south Texas, yellow blooms topped tall yucca. In the desert of Big Bend National Park, the ocotillo spread its red blooms atop black skeletal stalks. Along the gulf coast, ocean smells floated into open car windows on magnolia-scented breezes. In Alabama, an azalea jungle was conquering an abandoned house. Georgia and North Carolina displayed graceful splashes of white dogwood in variegated greening woods. We drove north into Virginia and watched the dogwood thin and curl back into buds as in a film run in reverse. We arrived in Washington, D. C., to see the cherry blossoms peak.

I tried desperately to imprint all that color on my memory so that I could later superimpose it against bare trees and brown hillsides. We arrived home, packed away the shorts and sandals and re-donned sweatshirts and boots only to discover that the earth had seemingly not changed one bit. Our world had budged not one whit closer to green in the weeks we'd been gone. Running away didn't seem to be the answer.

I've now spent a few of these seasons here, and I'm slowly coming to the conclusion that perhaps the "something wrong" is me. How I cling to my old perception of what spring should be. Yesterday on the street I met a cheery old friend. "Isn't spring wonderful!" she called to me. It was snowing like crazy, but I'm trying to experience the season through her senses. I stopped to chat with a neighbor who was happily working to clean up her yard around receding snow banks. "It's spring!" she assured me. I'm trying hard to feel whatever she's feeling.

The mountains are still winter-clad. If I look up, I see a storybook alpine scene. When I look down, I do see that winter is on the run. Decks, bushes, along with all sorts of forgotten objects resurface in the afternoon warmth; the robin choir is practicing in the cottonwood; snowmelt beats lightly on the deck; a lone chipmunk darts out from under a bench on the boardwalk ‐ all hints that the real "it" will come someday.

This morning, I walked to the bank in a sunny, sweatshirt day. In the yard I walked on real ground ‐ granted, I didn't step on real green, but there is plant life where summer's grass will someday be. Looking ever so closely, I found three greenish clovers in the squishy ground under a tree. I stepped onto a dry deck to fetch the ice skates and skis, and putting them away in the garage, I wondered where the real winter went. By early afternoon, we let the fire go out, and we may not have to build another one tonight.

On the first sunny Sunday afternoon in this season that follows winter, we drove out to Lake San Cristobal. The townsfolk had hit the outdoors like troops landing for an invasion. What the sun and warm temperatures do to the snow is nothing compared with what they do for our spirits. It might as well be spring. Teenagers donned shorts and tank tops, yet sudden wind gusts could whip up a good crop of goose bumps.

The lake was still a white blanket, topstitched by game tracks. A scattering of curled augers, a scurry of curious dogs and splotches of color marking distant ice fishermen decorated the white. Open lawn chairs dotted the sun-glistened surface, their occupants in rolled-up sleeves with faces turned skyward. Above the lake, cross-country skiers glided along the road as smoothly as rowboats. On the other side, bicycles bobbed along dry pavement at steady intervals.

Though we could see them as nothing more than specks from our vantage point on the lake, we knew that on top of "71" mountain, the snowmobilers had killed their engines, looked down on our world, and ate their sandwiches in mountaintop bliss. The mountain is nicknamed "71" because the crevices of snow which linger into summer form the numbers "71", which are visible for miles. We call it "our" mountain because we first came to Lake City in 1971. We have no doubt that nature has provided us our personal, permanent reminder.

Back home in town, we rejoiced in the fact that all we can do in this great weather is play in it. There's far too much snow left to rake the lawn. It's too muddy to tackle outdoor clean up. No need to wash the car, and besides, the hose is still hibernating. Garden planting is a good two months away. It's much too cool to paint. Nothing to do but pick your fun and go for it.

Oh, I haven't totally made my peace with this season. I still feel a surge of anger when I awaken to see white roofs in May. Yet, even I can sense that spring storms have a whole different feel from winter ones. Last week, I watched the sky break its blue promise, turn grey and whip up a snowstorm in an instant. It started like others of late - blustery little showers interspersed with momentary bursts of sunshine. But suddenly this one became credible. It was heavy and persistent, piling up quickly on tree limbs and windshields and mounding bushes in no time. The storm's will weakened my initial outrage at yet another violation of spring. Sleep came that night listening to the familiar crunch of tires in new snow. And then the morning! Quiet and warm under a fresh blue sky. Early sun lit gems everywhere. Snow clumps clung to bare aspen limbs like patches of cotton. In no other version of spring have I heard a stronger chorus of birds. Maybe they're befuddled at the world they'd come back to. Maybe they sang from sheer glee at this spectacle in white. Then the sun started its rapid attack, and in minutes it began to peel away the snow. Now that I've been through the cycle of seasons up here, I know what's coming, or more important, I know that "it" will come; "it" will eventually make its subtle slow appearance. We'll see the faintest, ever-so-slight beginning of a hint of a tinge of green on grey aspen groves. Here and there, we'll spot a splotch of yellow dandelion; on the brush along the river, a pale golden glow. And one day, the whir of a hummingbird.

Perhaps spring comes so slowly and gently up here so that we may truly grasp it. After all those months of winter, we need some convincing. No parades, no theatrics, no explosions. Just a quiet unfolding. You must appreciate something that you have to look for so closely and wait for so long.

Nevertheless, I'm not putting away the shovel just yet.

The Season Of The Mud

Most folks who live up here year 'round
Would call this place divine.
Tourists dub it paradise -
Perfection down the line.

The summer's like a brilliant dream;
In fall the aspens glow;
The snow creates a fairyland -
There's one more season, though:

The one we never talk about,
Our secret's kept in tow
Our unspoken convenant.
The world will never know

That when the snow begins to melt
Before a single bud
Preceding any aspen shoot:
THE SEASON OF THE MUD.

Euphemizing is our game,
We know that's all it takes,
That northern state can't outdo us:
Town of Ten Thousand Lakes.

Reflecting pools are what they are -
Mirrors for our peaks.
Abstract designs by tires and boots
Textures, swirls and streaks.

We don't admit that cars and trucks
All turn the same brown hue
That dogs and boots and children's feet
Track in the slimy goo.

We're stoic as cattle in the slush
That calmly chew their cud,
A springtime pastoral undisturbed
By udders mired in mud.

When March and April come around
And plant life's still inert,
We yearn to glimpse the greening grass

Beneath this liquid dirt.
We trust that those who read these lines
Won't leak a single thing
About our secret fluid sod
When elsewhere it is spring.

The Night The Lights Went Out

 We used Bob's grandmother's old kerosene lamp as a prop in our old-time portrait studio. During one spring, pre-opening cleaning, I'd brought the lamp to the kitchen for a globe shining. Little did I know that it would be put to its real use that evening.

For days, Colorado had been trapped in a messy rainy system. Late afternoon had been indescribable to anyone not familiar with capricious mountain weather. Blowing snowstorms looked earnestly like winter while sudden bursts of sunshine broke though shouting, "All's well! Spring is here!" Raging winds slapped loose objects around town, and misty, haunting clouds encircled the valley, wiping out all signs of the surrounding peaks as if a playful artist had simply brushed the mountains away.

A slow steady rain had begun. The insular evening lured us to put another log on the fire and settle in for some mindless hours, to loop back and enjoy one more winter's eve. On the television, Matlock had just picked up on his first substantial clue when, blooey! The television blanked, the microwave squealed and the lights went out.

For a time we sat patiently expecting the momentary return of our lifeline. After an hour, we decided that this could be a power failure of substance and rounded up fresh flashlight batteries, candles and matches.

Then we noticed it on the counter, poised for the rescue: great grandma's lamp. It worked fine. I settled down intending to read the hours away until the lights came on. I soon discovered that the dim, jerky flame barely lit the shape of the book, let alone the letters on the page. So much for the romance of a "Little House on the Prairie" evening with everyone gathered around the lamp reading, studying, sewing.

I grew restless. Popcorn would taste great, except that the stove and microwave were electric. I had tons of typing to do, but the typewriter was electric (pre-computer days). I could iron the rest of those old-time costumes...I could bake the muffins I'd planned to make tomorrow...finish vacuuming...run the baskets of laundry....

What on earth did those people do on a Tuesday evening up here 100 years ago?

Outside the sky gradually darkened. Clouds still claimed the mountains. Our little village sat dark and motionless. In the dim lamplight, familiar objects took on strange shapes. Hanging plants cast eerie, jungle-like shadows on the ceiling. Pacing the house, I looked out each window. Nothing stirred. Never, even in the midst of a winter snowfall, had the town seemed so still.

Then I noticed, one by one in neighboring buildings, a faint flickering began. No fully-lit panes, no streetlights, no flood's glare, only a small soft yellow glow in the windows, barely visible and quietly reassuring.

I stood looking out the window at each flickering light. For a moment, I had a fleeting sense of what the settlers' lives had been like. I couldn't sustain it, of course, but for an instant, something connected with the past.

The Lake City Summertime Hustle

 Chances are if somebody just happened into town for the first time, they wouldn't pick up on it. If they've been around awhile, however, they would recognize the beat right away. It's a number that hits the charts annually at this time of year.

It's called The Lake City Hustle.

Sure, we knew all along that summer was around the corner, that the tourists were coming back. Yet it's not until the lady who drives the mail from Gunnison warns us that the first ones have passed through The Gate and are approaching town that we really start moving to the Hustle. One day we're still stopping for long mid-street conversations with neighbors, still happily chipping away at that winter project that we started in April, and the next day, we're racing like characters in a cartoon chase. Doing the Hustle.

Paint that trim, build those shelves, move that dirt, polish those windows, price that stock, clean that flowerbed. Even folks who don't have businesses catch the beat to get their personal world in order before they start working three summer jobs.

Before I lived here full time, I saw no good reason for those people to wait until the last minute to prepare for summer. Didn't they know it was coming? All this haste was counterproductive. What did they do all winter anyway?

Little did I know.

At sometime during the winter, most of us seriously consider getting a head start on summer. But there are those gloriously sunny, warm days that shout at you to ski them, and those rare but luscious misty ones that threaten to snowbound you and beg you to snuggle by the fire with a book. More consuming, however, are the day-to-day responsibilities of holding the town together, of tackling the significant tasks that keep us alive and moving as a community, jobs that get short shrift in summer. Little did I know.

Mostly, however, I never realized the enormity of work that must necessarily wait until early summer. It's hard to dig in frozen ground. It's no fun to rake yards and wash windows in sharp winds that threaten to blow up a storm any minute. In other parts of the country, people can start those jobs anywhere from February to April while we're prudently counting the last of our firewood.

So be gone, guilt. We came here to enjoy life, and we've enjoyed the winter. It wasn't our doing that those blustery, wintry days lasted too long. Now the grass is greening, the dandelions are sprouting and the tourists are coming.

So come on everybody, let's do the Hustle!

Whatever else summer may be up here, it is fleeting. It's like a rich, delicious ice cream cone: try as you may, you cannot savor it all before the ice cream starts to melt away.

Summer is a bittersweet whirlwind. All those delightful people to meet and enjoy, friendships to renew and strengthen, the fun-

packed calendar to take in, miles of trails to hike, good restaurants to eat our way through - all coming at once when we have the least time to savor them. How I've wished that the Summer Circus could come to town just once for a day or two in the middle of March.

For a time each year, I doubt that summer will ever return. However, sometime by the end of June, ready or not, those stark grey aspen start spinning full-leafed in the sunshine. Overnight, dandelions erupt and ripple through town. Cottonwood fluff dusts the streets, and vegetable gardens sprout rows of yellow and green fringe. When it began one year, I wrote these lines:

Opening The Pass

Where they plowed the jeep road

I hike through snow banks taller than I am

Giant slices of marbled soil and snow

Layered with pine-needle coconut.

On the jeep road

Spring run-off

Silvers tire ruts and boot treads

And ordinary ditches spawn waterfalls.

In early summer, Henson Creek and the Lake Fork of the Gunnison attack the valley, rushing, shouting, charging the road. I love to walk along Henson Creek, scan the banks for the first sprinkle of red firecracker blossoms and welcome the faithful primrose unfurling in the rocks. Delicate wild iris beds herald summer with gentle lavender strokes in green marshes.

"Opening!" sounds everywhere. Opening night at the Black Crooke Theatre. Opening of bingo, restaurants, motels, shops and summer events. Openings blossom like wildflowers.

On the Fourth of July, hordes of people fill Silver Street and the town park, a sharp contrast to our winter quiet. The street fills with dancers; the lyrics of "Rocky Mountain Rainbow" lift from the flatbed truck to warm the chilly air. Residents and visitors lock arms and sing spontaneously about America and freedom while the fireworks spray the mountain.

In summer, we cook out with friends, watch tumultuous pink and orange sunsets reflect on Lake San Cristobal and sometimes stay late enough to look at the dazzling canopy of stars. I love to walk through River Fork Campground at dusk and chat with folks in front of their trailers and smell their group campfire. I cherish fleeting visits from family and friends and face the residue of things we didn't have time to do and the things we didn't say. I say "Hello" and "See you next year" to a stream of annual visitors.

Summer means hiking in deep woods along a singing stream. It means breaking out into a meadow of color, sun slapping the back of your neck, and climbing to the velvet silence of a high mountain lake. It means breathing air so clean that it bathes your lungs.

I was looking for something in a book of quotations recently when these words jumped out at me; "Our life is frittered away by detail." It was Thoreau, of course, reminding me of things I tend to ignore. Summer brings with it the annual "detail versus trail" conflict.

How to juggle all the details and still salvage time to remember why we live here? There is, after all, a living to be earned and projects that can't be completed in frozen ground. Commitments don't melt away with the snow, and responsibilities don't disappear just because the lake has thawed and the hummingbirds are back.

So many trails to hike and peaks to scale. So many streams to fish and sit by. So little time. The ice cream is dripping.

LICK!

One glorious July day, a couple of friends and I decided to hike to Sloan Lake, and if we felt courageous enough, we'd follow the trail on up to the top of Handies Peak, one of five mountains in our immediate area over 14,000 feet high. The trail to Sloan Lake climbs slightly upward through American Basin with its floor of assorted wildflowers, then steeply up past timberline to breathtaking views of neighboring mountains, streams and stark grey rock cliffs. As we hiked toward Sloan Lake, we savored, as we always do, the amazing variety of tundra flowers - miniscule, delicate and fleeting. In town, summer was well on its way, but we'd probably find Sloan still partially iced in. Along the high valley stream, marsh marigolds were just beginning to push through soggy grasses. Such struggle for a few weeks' life in the sun.

On the way to Sloan, a couple of youngsters passed us, attacking the steep trail at a pace that tired us to watch. One girl was holding a tuft of moss campion large enough to cover both palms. For a moment we stared, incredulous at the velvety green and bright pink cushion in her hands. The fact that she'd ripped up a handful of rare tundra blooms stopped us in our tracks. Finally, Susan found her voice. She was unmerciful, but she gave vent to all our feelings.

"Do you know that those flowers can take up to 200 years to grow? This country had hardly begun when that clump started. And now it won't live. It will only die out of its home."

The girl ducked her head, but didn't say a word to us. I'm sure she meant no harm but was simply ignorant of the seriousness of what she'd done.

Little did I know that later that day, I myself would be ripping tundra from the mountainside.

By the time we reached the lake, we were both tired and energized. Only on high mountain hikes have I experienced that paradox. There's a magic afoot up there that urges you to keep going, to climb higher, even though your body screams that it needs more air. Handies Peak towered above Sloan Lake. It might as well have said, "Climb me! Climb me!"

The trail up Handies is better marked today than it was then; nevertheless, I'll never know how we missed it. Talking probably, possibly simply mesmerized by the view. When we realized our mistake, our choices were to backtrack - the day was moving on too swiftly, and we knew the rule about being on the top of any Fourteener as early as possible - or to simply scale the slope and pick up the switchback trail farther up. How three grown women could lose their minds simultaneously is beyond me, but we did. It looked climbable. We started up the slope.

The first hundred yards or so were walkable, and we smugly congratulated ourselves on being such brave mountain women.

Suddenly the grade pitched. Instinct brought us to our hands and knees. Rock after rock proved rotten in our grip, like loose teeth. The soil was corn-meal soft.

I looked at the only feasible foothold - outcroppings of buttercup bushes, tiny delicate, lustrous blossoms with roots embedded in the guts of the mountain. I froze.

"Come on! Brace your foot on the bush!" Jo called. I couldn't move. She offered me her hand; I took it, and dug my boot against the delicate bloom.

Time and time again, I thrust my foot against one clump, forced my body forward while my hand clutched Jo's for leverage. Between each push, my thoughts paralyzed me. "This is where I'm going to die. They couldn't even land a rescue helicopter on this slope. God, how I hate to tear up these flowers."

"Come on!" Jo repeated, and I pushed again. Incongruously, I thought of the rhythm of childbirth pains and pushes.

Carving each foothold in the mealy earth, we ascended by inches, bush by bush. Bellying against soil, my universe stretched only from buttercup to buttercup. I tried not to look down the vertical slope, but it drew my eyes, and each glance told me there was no compromise, no ledge, no chance to reclaim the distance. Nothing between us and the valley floor except strewn rotten rocks. And buttercups.

Gradually the terrain released us. Shaking on two feet, we looked back. The buttercup slope was so steep it vanished beneath us.

I've been up Handies Peak several times, but this was the only day that it remained bright and clear at the top. We stretched out in the sunshine for at least an hour. Occasionally we spoke. I'm glad I was able to thank Jo for saving my life. She died a few years later.

But mostly we were quiet, alone with our own thoughts.

Every summer as we enjoy temperatures that seldom reach out of the seventies, tales of heat waves across the country reach Lake City. One such day, I remembered something that happened to me on a hot day in the South.

I was staying at a motel in the midst of the historic district of Charleston, South Carolina. The motel's swimming pool was a tiny oval tucked at the back of the rooms behind the parking lot, a motel's length away from the office and separated from an adjoining alley by a brick lattice wall. Three young boys had arrived before I did, and their raucous splashes pretty well occupied the whole pool.

I relaxed in the sun with my book, choosing neither to dampen their fun nor to be churned around in their wake. Time after time, they hoisted themselves out of the pool, backed up as far as they could past the "No Diving" sign in order to make the greatest possible splash with their running dives.

The mother in me stirred uneasily. "Why didn't their own parents come out and decide if they were doing something dangerous?" The child in me celebrated the sheer glee and abandonment with which they attacked the water and each other.

Each time they approached my chair, they carefully slowed to a walk and said, "Excuse me." They moved their most rambunctious games to the far side of the pool and turned occasionally to check that their splashes were not reaching me. Beyond that, there was no hesitation in their play. It was loud, physical and relentless.

Finally they emerged from the pool somewhat reluctantly. I glanced up, expecting to see them turn toward the motel rooms. Instead, they scaled the lattice brick wall; the openings made easy footholds. When they looked at me, they showed only the faintest hint of wariness. They sat talking atop the wall for a while, long enough for their swimsuits to stop dripping, I suppose.

Then, pulling jeans, t-shirts and shoes from a recessed hiding place in the wall, they dressed leisurely and made their way down the back side of the latticed brick into the alley.

I was totally surprised by their ruse.

Not far from the historic district, I remembered having driven through some of the most depressing slums I'd ever seen. Crowded, ramshackle houses sat right on the street with no space for play. The whole neighborhood had looked steamy and hot. I didn't know where the boys had come from, but I could speculate.

I made peace with my conscience. No, I was not single-handedly leading them further down the path of deception and on to a life of crime. I quelled my annoyance that my exorbitant motel bill was subsidizing their play.

It had been a joyous, memorable afternoon for a trio of youngsters who more than likely would never stick a toe in a clear mountain stream or feel the cooling breeze off an alpine lake.

As their checkered figures cleared the lattice wall, they hesitated, caught my eye and waved goodbye in unison, sealing our secret and their trust.

There's an anecdote attributed to one of the old-timers that goes something like this: when asked what people do up here in the summer, the old-timer allegedly replied, "Well, if it comes on Sunday, we pitch horseshoes."

Whatever else summer brings, it can bring rain. Usually it comes in predictable, playful afternoon showers. They vanish as quickly as they come, and leave us to go on about whatever summer business we were up to. Some summers, however, seem to be one perpetual rainfall with a couple of days of clear weather thrown in. Shorts are laundered once or twice while the sweatshirts, fleecy robe and wooly socks get a workout. Once I counted twenty days since we'd had fair weather. Not that it rained for twenty days solid (after all, that's half a flood) but there was that persistent threat: that perpetual mist overtaking the momentary burst of blue sky.

At first a July-morning woodstove fire is a novelty. Something to write about to folks sweltering in three-digit degrees. After a while, though, impatience sets in followed by an urgency for skies to clear, then a near-panic that the precious summer is slipping away.

Compared to other places, my former home among them, grey rainy days are not a tremendous contrast to familiar bland skies. But here! We're just not used to them. They become the subject of all conversation: the trails are muddy; the passes are slippery; moisture gnaws at narrow shelf roads; streams are high; snow banks block paths into favorite spots. Cookouts are canceled; campers pack up wet duds and move to town, or somewhere else, or home. Town puddles become lake-like and permanent. Our spirits slump and our nerves get edgy.

At such times, I'm grateful for our visiting vacationers – they keep the world in perspective. Just when I'm thinking if I were visiting here, I'd never come back, they say, "It's wonderful! We love it! It never rains where we're from!" I stand in the gallery door and watch them stroll the streets in their raingear, soaking up the cool. They fish in it. They jeep in it.

Finally, inevitably, the sun does return. It restores texture to the slopes; it creates deep green cloud-shadows on meadows; it dries puddles and tents and sleeping bags; it warms deckchairs and car seats. It penetrates sweatshirts and once again caresses bare arms.

Once a summer, or at least every few summers, we're also hit by a serious hailstorm. I've been reminded of Robert Frost's lines:

"The rain to the wind said

"you push and I'll pelt"

And they so smote the garden wall

That the flowers actually knelt

And lay lodged, though not dead...

The pelting hail shreds flowers and turn streets winter-white in minutes. The sudden drop in temperature seals the ice pebbles in place. Hours later, rooftops are still white, and even the next day, northerly areas may still be edged in white.

After one such memorable hailstorm, Bob and I drove high into the mountains. "What's wrong with this picture?" I asked as I looked at white ditches bordering Henson Creek road in August.

At the entry to the woods, summer grasses glistened through a lacy white coverlet. Felled green aspen leaves carpeted the path as only gold ones are supposed to do. Icy filigree trimmed rocks and

log edges. Scraggly lavender aster reached up through the ice-pebble beds. One tiny, fragile harebell, barely born, turned toward the sun, hoping for a bit of a lifetime. Deep in the woods, the thin white layer crunched underfoot with the sound of winter.

Nearby, a pool of melted hail, still and seamless as the day, reflected sharp-edged cumulus portending more of the same. Like winter, summer is also a tease, ignoring the calendar, bringing us whatever weather it chooses.

The freak cold days leave, and summer always returns. We hope.

Nevertheless, just in case, I may round up a game of horseshoes for Sunday.

One day in summer, someone pushes the fast-forward button. I'm convinced that some year scientists will reveal that a mysterious phenomenon has been accelerating the months of June, July and August above 8,000 feet. In the midst of its clamor, someone must have secretly declared that they'd be glad when "it" was over. Curses upon them! Like a fairy tale wish uttered, the light flashed, the thunder boomed and poof! Summer is ending.

Even the brightest sunny days have a cool edge. There's a bit of frost on the windshield early mornings. The lighting on the slopes is turned down a notch, revealing detail and contrast that had been lost in the harsher brightness. Feeling worrisome, I bring in the geraniums for a safer night. Cabins are bundled up with boards. Firewood stacks grow daily. Crossing the highway in town is no longer a challenge, and you can see around the corner at stop signs. The brilliant fuchsia fireweed that colored curves along the road is all stalk. The carnival of color gives way to summer's last hues – smatterings of gold and purple petals, a regal, if understated, finale. I decide that I probably shouldn't refill the hummingbird feeder. Around town, "One more show" and "Last Night" become the theme. The dead-give-away behavior starts: singles start moving in together, their choices often dominated by evaluating who has the largest woodpile.

Robert Frost said it all in one poem title, "Happiness Makes Up in Height for What it Lacks in Length."

The Alferd Packer Summer

One July, a few years after I retired here, a team of scientists along with the national media descended on Lake City to exhume the bodies of Alferd Packer's victims. Should there be anyone left on earth who hasn't heard of Alferd Packer, he was the leader of a prospecting group that in the winter of 1874 was forced to camp on the banks of the Lake Fork of the Gunnison River near what is today Lake City. Even after the exhumation, colloquially referred to around here as "The Dig," scholars still debate the intricacies of the case. Packer has gone down in history, corroborated by the scientists who conducted The Dig, as the cannibal who ate the rest of his group to survive the winter.

In the late fall of 1873, Packer had joined a prospecting group in Utah whose purpose was to find gold in the San Juans. Early in 1874, the twenty-one-man party reached Chief Ouray's camp at the junction of Dry Creek and the Uncompahgre River near where Delta, Colorado, stands today. The Indian chief strongly advised the men not to go into the mountains in winter. No doubt growing restless waiting for spring, Packer and five companions ignored Ouray's warning and started into the San Juans. Their provisions would last probably only about seven days, but that seemed sufficient, as their destination was the Los Pinos Indian Agency. They became lost and ended up camping on the Lake Fork.

In mid-April, Alferd Packer walked into the Los Pinos Indian Agency, alone, looking well fed and telling a story about becoming separated from his fellow travelers. His victims' bodies were subsequently found, and Packer was detained in the Saguache jail. Before he could be charged and tried, however, he escaped from the jail and was not heard from for nine years. Then he was apprehended in Wyoming and brought to trial in Lake City in 1883.

On Friday, April 13, the jury declared Packer guilty of murder and sentenced him to hang. Thus was born one of the famous legends about Lake City. A local saloon keeper, Larry Dolan, burst into the streets of Lake City, claiming to quote Judge Melville B. Gerry as he yelled, "...they was seven dimmycrats in Hinsdale County, and ye eat five 'em!" In truth, Judge Gerry's statement was serious and moving. A legal technicality canceled Packer's execution in Lake City; he was later tried and convicted in Gunnison.

Today, visitors climb the stairs to the Hinsdale County courtroom and sit in the same chairs that trial spectators occupied in 1883. Two faculty members from the nearby state college in Gunnison wrote and produced a play, *The Last Trial of Alferd Packer*, which has been performed several summers in the courtroom.

For over one hundred years, Lake City quietly harbored its mystery. Oh, you could buy T-shirts at The General Store that read, "Have a Friend for Dinner" and an Alferd Packer feast has been an annual tradition at the University of Colorado's cafeteria. In spite of Lake City's, "Alferd Packer Days," an annual event that has included cook-offs and coffin races, most residents believe that we have greater claims to fame than a renowned cannibal.

Nevertheless, In July of 1989, prefaced by months of national media coverage, a team of scientists dug up the victims' remains in search of answers to one of the country's most perplexing crimes. Earlier that year, I interviewed James E. Starrs, leader of The Dig in his office at George Washington University in Washington, D.C. Starrs had long been fascinated by the unsettled questions of the case. So, he assembled the scientific team consisting of archeologists, anthropologists, a firearms examiner, and a pathologist, and along with the national media, invaded Lake City. Following the exhumation, the excavated remains were sent to the University of Arizona for microscopic examination. The bones were returned to Lake City, and a proper burial service was held for them with a large crowd attending and ministers of five faiths all blessing them. The main thing I remember about that day was trying to stifle my amusement when one of the ministers proclaimed, "Man shall not live by bread alone." I'll never know if the irony was on purpose or not.

Even after the official, scientific verdict that Packer had indeed attacked and eaten his companions, several years later, a nearby college professor raised new questions, and the controversy flamed again.

By and large, the residents here marked time while the bones were dug and reburied. We now knew what it meant to be courted by national media, praised by many, and put down by some.

"What can you possibly do to top this event?" a visitor asked. I felt pretty confident that the mountains, streams, blue skies and great neighbors would still be here after the Packer pandemonium. Of course, we were pleased that a lot of new people had found us for whatever reasons. I'm sure that many of them have come back.

We were properly proud to have science advanced in our environs. And we had a lot of fun in the process.

A Lake City Thing To Do

 Lisa Bowers had vacationed with her parents in Lake City for thirteen summers. After becoming engaged to Roger Harbart, it followed that she would have to bring him to see Lake City. Lisa and Roger arrived for a brief vacation, and Roger fell in love with Lake City at first sight, just as Lisa had many years before.

The couple had planned a big December wedding in Texas. On the evening of August 20, however, while looking at the stars up Henson Creek Road, their wedding plans abruptly changed. They vowed that if all the pieces could fall into place in one day, they would be married the next evening in Lake City's First Baptist Church, "the little white church on the hill" which Lisa had described to Roger before he came to Lake City.

Friday morning dawned with the list of tasks facing them. They made arrangements for the minister, the church and the marriage license, and then they learned that they would have to go to Gunnison for blood tests. With only hours left in their Friday wedding day, they traveled the sixty miles to Gunnison. They were told that pre-marital blood tests were done only on Thursdays.

Lisa broke into tears. In typical Western Slope style, a humane phone call or two cut through the tape, and they took the necessary tests. Clerks warned Lisa that she'd never find a veil in town, but a florist created one, along with a delicate wild iris and white rosebud bouquet for the bride and the groom's white bud boutonniere. They had hoped for a specially baked wedding cake, but time proved too short. They chose a Pepperidge Farms frozen one.

We became involved with the wedding plans when the breathless couple popped into our place to ask if my husband could photograph the ceremony. Bob explained that he had an outdoor portrait appointment, and then he had to set up for bingo in the armory. He would, however, do his best to be at the church by 6:15.

"Do you think you could find a pianist?" Lisa asked me. I immediately called Edie Swanson, resident pianist and lover of special events, knowing that she would fully share their joy.

Before the ceremony, Edie filled the sanctuary with "The hills are alive with the sound of music." The bride wore a stylish navy and white stunningly coordinated outfit that she must have packed for some special vacation event.

Reverend Fluker, the Baptist minister, graciously took time from his busy day at his Phillips station "day job" and changed from his gas-pumping coveralls into a dignified grey suit. Nine people, including Bob and me, shared the event. The other seven, including the witnesses, were people that Lisa and Roger had met during the week at the Texan Resort where they were staying.

A light, early evening shower started as Lisa and Roger posed by their car for a get-away shot. Reverend Fluker rushed back to the gas station to handle Friday evening traffic. Edie returned to her gift shop in the Swanson House, and Bob and I went to check on bingo. The seven Texan neighbors went their own way.

I suppose we all had our reasons for getting involved with Lisa and Roger. Mainly, it just seemed like the Lake City thing to do.

Beyond that though, I recalled an afternoon in a restaurant overlooking the Boston Mountains in northern Arkansas. We were engaged and planning a wedding many months hence. The mountain's magic, youth's impulsiveness, whatever, took over and two days later we were married. That was many years ago.

We hoped that Lisa and Roger would fare at least as well.

Why "Black Crooke?"

 At the corner of Third and Silver Streets, the crossroads of downtown Lake City, stands the Black Crooke Theatre, a building that has become the heartbeat of much community life. Schoolchildren, locals and visitors alike have asked why in the world it has such a strange name. One visitor was so offended by the name that she refused to attend any event in the venue.

In 1880, at the peak of Lake City's booming mining days, John Hough built an impressive brick structure that is still called the Hough Building. From his two-story mercantile building, Hough supplied virtually every need of the surrounding Lake City miners.

Almost a century later, John H. Parker II arrived in Lake City from Parkersburg, West Virginia, and purchased not only the Hough Building, but several other downtown buildings as well. In the 1970s, Parker performed extensive renovation of the Hough Building including the transformation of one corner of the first floor into a theatre to house live productions. He named the space The Black Crooke Theatre.

According to Parker, the name was suggested by the late Smoky Swanson, a long-time local character whose choice teems with legend and history. The name is a creative combination from three sources.

The first was one of the most significant milestones in American theatre. In 1866, two New York producers had imported a Parisian ballet troupe to perform at the Academy of Music in New York City. Before the show opened, however, the theatre burned to the ground and the producers were left with a high-priced company of idle dancers. They approached the manager of Niblo's Garden who was planning to produce a melodrama called *The Black Crook*. The playwright's need for money convinced him to allow the combination of the two shows, even though he objected to the desecration of his work. *The Black Crook* became the costliest, most ornate and most daring show Americans had ever seen.

Clad in short skirts and flesh-colored tights, a hundred women danced and leapt across the stage. Special effects – scenes rising out of the floor, fairies flying through the air, glistening stalagmites and stalactites in a crystal grotto, a hurricane of gauze – dazzled audiences unlike anything previously created on the American stage. Theatre goers had never seen anything like it.

The title, *The Black Crook*, came from the swarthy Herzog, the lead character in the original melodrama, the "black" having nothing to do with his race and everything to do with his character. In the Faustian-like plot, Herzog contracts to deliver one soul a year to the devil in exchange for an additional year of life and magical powers.

The initial *Black Crook* engagement ran an unprecedented 474 performances that lasted sixteen months. In the next two decades it was revived eight times in New York, and touring companies performed it constantly throughout the country. *The Black Crook* was a landmark production in show business in America, laying the groundwork for both the burlesque show and musical comedy. Some people acclaim *The Black Crook* as the first musical comedy.

Meanwhile in the Wild West, a group of fortune-seeking miners in remote Hinsdale County named a set of mines after this popular show. They were called "The Black Crook Group." Thus, the second source for the theatre's curious name.

About the same time as The Black Crook Group explorations, John J. Crooke, who incidentally invented tin foil, built and operated Crooke's smelter at Crooke's Falls, just south of Lake City. In 1976, John Parker chose the *Crooke* spelling when naming his newly renovated theatre.

Over the next twenty years, the Black Crooke Theatre housed a variety of community functions. In 1992, the Lake City Arts Council leased the theatre that now serves as a community arts center.

Unbeknownst to Herzog or the hundred skimpily clad dancers, certainly unbeknownst to the world-wise miners, the Black Crooke Theatre in Lake City, Colorado, has had many an additional year of life. Some even believe, given the explosion of creativity that occurs within its walls, that the theatre has magical powers.

Officer Down

 It was pre-dawn on the morning of November 18, 1994. Bob always gets up and goes downstairs before me. He hurried back upstairs and awakened me to tell me the news. In the darkness of the room and through the grogginess of my mind, I struggled to hear him.

"The Hinsdale County Sheriff has been murdered. It was just on Channel 9!"

I couldn't focus. It took me a few seconds to think who our sheriff was.

"Oh my God," I finally realized, "It's Roger."

I grabbed a robe and scurried downstairs to listen for more television news and the horror transmitted on our local scanner. Originally appointed to fill out another sheriff's term, Roger Coursey had been elected by a two-to-one margin only days before.

In the midst of the crisis, I couldn't think tidily; thoughts and emotions tumbled together in ragged pieces. Only later did I realize the progression: first came absolute disbelief. This can't be happening in our peaceful little town. Nobody shoots people here. Fear followed the denial: those murderers are still somewhere around here. And finally: what should we be doing to help?

During the morning the story unraveled and the mystery intensified. The Mineral County Sheriff, just over the mountain in Creede, had radioed that the perpetrators of an attempted bank robbery, a man and a woman, were heading our way. Then, the sheriff and his undersheriff stopped a truck at the base of Slumgullion Pass, just south of town. They walked up to the truck, the sheriff to the driver's side. The driver aimed a gun and shot him. The truck sped off; the undersheriff fired several shots at the vehicle. The sheriff died instantly.

Soon the damaged truck was found abandoned on a road off the highway, a short distance from the scene of the shooting. Our fear increased. Either the couple was on foot or they had arranged for get-away transportation. That didn't seem feasible - they couldn't have anticipated the pressing need to escape so quickly. How could they have made arrangements that rapidly? Could it have been coincidence that they had planned to be picked up in Lake City?

Dogs traced the scent, hither and yon, to the north end of town, up and down mountainsides. Snow that had fallen the night before gave a few track clues. In the meantime, authorities worked to clear every empty house and outbuilding in the area - no small task with the number of summer homes here. Ordinary citizens joined law enforcement to search and clear houses and businesses in town. They urged residents to stay inside with doors locked. All morning we followed their directions, ears tuned to the scanner while we eyed the Denver television station.

In no time, the killers had been identified - thanks to a roll of undeveloped film left in the truck and a prescription for an anti-depressant medicine. "Wanted" bulletins bearing their descriptions ripped across the country.

Sheriffs, state patrolmen, deputies and SWAT teams from all over Colorado bustled into town. Over 150 people came to help. The local armory, normally used as a gym and community center, now housed troops; cots lined the basketball court, and rifles leaned against the bleachers.

Cameras flashed, reporters filled notebooks, and television vans from as far away as Denver arrived. Words and pictures appeared everywhere - in newspapers and on television screens across the country. Every angle of the story was explored and often exploited.

The community sprang into action. I added my turkey noodle soup to the pots and casseroles crowding the Presbyterian Church's kitchen counter where visiting officers and media gathered to eat. Neighbors strapped pistols around their waists. Some women volunteered to go scrub the blood off the highway.

What was one more fleeting violent headline to people across the nation had devastated our small, closely-knit community.

Most of us could tell stories of the energetic law enforcement officer whom we felt so lucky to have. Only a few days before, he had sat in our living room - no specific reason for the visit that I can remember. He was constantly making contact with the people he served; this time, he was the proud father telling of his son's journalistic achievements in the U. S. Army.

On my desk, the envelope had been stashed aside with the last several days' mail. It was postmarked November 14. The message inside read:

Dear Mary and Bob,

Thank you for your support and contribution to my election. I hope we can share in a good positive future in the years to come. Thank you again.

Roger

Weeks later, yellow plastic ribbons with black lettering still fluttered on doorknobs in morning breezes. These remnants of ugly, tragic days indicated that the building had been "cleared." Indeed, the buildings had all been "cleared."

Our hearts and minds, however, had not been cleared.

Weeks after Roger's murder, when newspaper and television headlines had turned to newer violence, we were still a community on the verge of tears. An innocent "Good Morning" could end in a wordless embrace. An unintentional remark unleashed a flood of images that we were collectively trying to put behind us.

Safety from the murderers was no longer the issue. A month later, their bodies had been found under a pine tree, on a mountainside just outside of town. They had taken their own lives, apparently on the same day they had committed the murder.

They had robbed us not only of a treasured person, but of our innocence as well. It was, admittedly, an innocence that bordered on complacency, even arrogance.

In the days following our tragedy, a Missouri newspaper carried this lead; "An order to lock doors during a manhunt for killers was tough for some residents of this historic mining town; it had been so long they couldn't find their keys."

While the article's tone was somewhat flippant for the gravity of our situation, it nevertheless captured our view of ourselves. Perhaps we'd been a little too smug as we heard stories of fear and crime in cities beyond The Gate. We liked to think that we were set apart from the "real world." We joked about life on the "outside."

Our loss of innocence went deeper than making sure we had keys to all our doors. It threatened something that had been fundamental to us: our trust.

Our easy and peaceful lifestyle has been built on trust. We've not only trusted each other, but we've trusted the thousands of strangers who walk into our shops, who sit in our restaurants, who fish our streams and camp in our outdoors.

On Thanksgiving Day that year, an out-of-state car stopped me while I was walking along Gunnison Avenue. The strangers simply wanted to find a gas station. Giving directions, answering visitors' questions are routine here. Yet, I felt momentarily uneasy, and I hated that feeling. I hated the idea that I had fleetingly wondered what they were doing here.

Strangers play an important role in our lives. Their visits are more than economic necessity; sharing this place with strangers is part of the fabric of our community. While we may complain about the summer madness, we know that the influx of strangers partially defines life here. Our openness and acceptance have been strengths.

After the murder, we often heard "Our little town will never be the same." The media have echoed that sentiment. We had to work together to keep that fear from becoming a self-fulfilling prophecy.

To be sure, trauma and loss change life. We have less control than we'd thought over what happens here, but we still have control over how we respond. Our innocence may have died with our sheriff, but we can retain our trust in each other as we try to rebuild our trust in the world outside - with which we are connected, like it or not.

I'll Let You Know

There was a period of time in which I didn't write much. I'd been busy organizing an arts council and a community theatre group, and my writing consisted largely of preparing grant proposals, tax-deductible applications and memos to new board members. A friend asked if I'd been lax in my writing because I'd been a full-time resident long enough to get used to it. The "it" would probably be vague to anyone who didn't live here, but I knew exactly what she meant.

Admittedly, I sometimes catch myself absorbed in the day's tasks ahead, oblivious to my surroundings. Admittedly, I sometimes have to remind myself to stop thinking and start looking. More often than not, however, when you're up here, you can't help looking. This place is possessed by wonder and surprise, and so long as they are at work, I'll never get used to it.

Not so long as the chipmunks perform their kamikaze dash-pause-dash routine across the road to some cartoon music score only they can hear. Their timing is truly comic.

Not so long as I can wonder each day what the lake will be like. Satin smooth, reflecting aspen, mirroring the tiny white boathouse?

Dark, vivid blue, echoing the sky? Jeweled and dazzling? Luscious aquamarine, a subtle blend no fashion designer can capture, white capped? All of the above?

I'll not get used to it so long as I can be surprised by a gentle doe staring at me, poised, velvet-like, in an arch of willows at the end of the lake. Or by the bronze marmot perched on the same rock at the highway's edge on three consecutive days. Or by a fawn innocently grazing among horses in a sun-bathed meadow.

Not so long as the sun strikes one last flaming patch of aspen centered in a forest already turned silver.

Or so long as I scrape frost off the windshield with numb fingers on a frosty mid-September morning and walk in shorts on a sunny mid-October afternoon.

Or, rounding a curve, I can see whether the peaks have more or less snow than the day before.

For years, I enjoyed a sizable patch of wild fuchsia fireweed blooming on our lot. Once, we bludgeoned its territory with construction activity, and I was sure that we'd destroyed the fireweed. Wrong. When its time came, there it was, coloring the late summer, taller and thicker than ever. I will not get used to it so long as those brilliant blossoms point to the sky.

I will not get used to it so long as balmy, suspenseful fall days stretch on and tantalize us with their secret of when the snow will come.

Should I get used to living here, I'll let you know.